Polish Cooking

...A cook is an artist creating impermanent works.
Fortunately, they sometimes
stay in our memory for a long time...

Mirosław Reszczyk

Polish cuisine is not a single, unchanging notion. The first Polish cookbook was written in 1682 (before King Sobieski's Vienna campaign!) In its introduction, the author, Stanisław Czerniecki, defended himself: "one should not feel offended that my first book begins with Polish dishes...". Western ways of cooking were already familiar to the Polish nobles' kitchens. For centuries Polish cuisine had absorbed and adapted French, Italian, Lithuanian and Jewish dishes. Oriental spices were not alien to it; some foreign vegetables and fruits brought by Queen Bona to Poland were widely accepted, competing with the native favorites –

cabbage, apples and pears.

Polish cuisine still thrives and grows, as it is simply everything Poles eat – in their home country and wherever they live around the world. Polish cuisine is an indispensable element of Polish culture and a marker of cultural and social development. It is spoken of mainly during traditional holidays and the meals associated with them, but every heart cherishes some favorite Polish dishes prepared by grandmother or mother for everyday meals. We come back to them eagerly, whether it be roll-ups, ryemeal soup, sauerkraut stew or crepes with farmer cheese and cherry preserves, because in this way we return to the family home of our childhood. We hope that you will find such recipes in this book, that you will refresh your memories of them and will pass their tradition to the next generation.

Appetizers, starter courses

Herring in oil 9

Herring (rollmops) 9

Carp in aspic 11

Jellied calf's or pig's feet 13

Steak tartare 15

Cooked vegetable salad 17

Spring salad 19

Tripe 21

Bean soup à la Brètonne 23

Bigos (meat & sauerkraut stew) 25

Herring in oil

inse herring (if very salty soak in cold water for an hour), slice into bite-size pieces or strips, place in a jar and cover with oil. Add spices. After 2–3 days the herring is perfect. It can be kept in the fridge for about 2 weeks (remember: the herring should remain covered with oil). Serve with finely chopped onion or onion slices, garnished with lemon, parsley or dill.

Herring (rollmops)

oak herring in water for 24 hours (change water several times). Cut off heads and remove gut, keep milt. Prepare fillets, remove bones, then spread each fillet with mustard, sprinkle with pepper and garnish with half the onion (chopped). Roll up chopped onion and pickles in each fillet, fasten with a toothpick and place in a jar. Boil vinegar with spices, the rest of the onion and water (proportion: 1 c. water to $\frac{1}{2}$ c. vinegar), then allow to cool. Remove sac from milt, rub milt through a sieve, mix with oil and combine with cooled vinegar marinade. Fill the jar of rolled herring with marinade, leave in the fridge for 2–3 days. Can be kept for 10 days in a cool place. Serve as an appetizer, or as a main course with baked potatoes.

Ingredients:

Herring in oil:
- 8 salt herring fillets
- 1 onion
- $\frac{1}{2}$ c. olive or sunflower oil
- 2–3 allspice seeds
- 2–3 peppercorns
- 1 bay leaf

Herring (rollmops):
- 4 whole salt herrings
- 2 pickles
- 1 large onion
- 1–2 T. prepared mustard
- wine vinegar (6%)
- bay leaf
- ground pepper
- sugar
- 2–3 T. olive or sunflower oil

Carp in aspic

cale and rinse carp. Remove gut, but do not rinse inside.
Fillet and salt. Leave for about half an hour.
Slice onion, clean and wash vegetables, carp head
and edible organs (liver, milt).
Put in a pot and add cold water (approx. 3 pt.).
Add spices and bring to a boil.
Place carp fillets in boiling bouillon and simmer 10–20 minutes
on a low flame. If fish is served on Christmas Eve,
place it on a deep platter, restoring its original shape
(including head). Strain fish stock (boil off if more than 1 pt.),
add salt and pepper to taste. Soak gelatin in a small quantity
of fish stock, add to the rest and mix.
Garnish with carrot (covering fish eye), cover with fish stock
and leave in a cool place until set.
Fillets may be served without the head, covered with aspic
and canned peas.
On Christmas Eve, carp is served with prepared horseradish
and white bread (preferably challah).

Ingredients:

- *2½ – 3 lb. carp*
- *3 large onions*
- *2 carrots*
- *2 parsnips*
- *a few allspice seeds and peppercorns*
- *2 bay leaves*
- *1 t. plain gelatin*
- *salt*
- *ground pepper*

Jellied calf's or pig's feet

*R*inse feet and split bones, rinse meat.
Clean, wash and cut vegetables and onion into large pieces.
Add bay leaves, allspice, peppercorns and garlic (best tied up
in cheesecloth). Add slightly salted water and simmer
on very low flame for 2 hours, until meat falls off the bones.
Take meat out, cut into small pieces, strain bouillon,
cover meat with bouillon, add salt and pepper to taste.
Add sliced carrots or arrange them in a jelling form previously
rinsed with cold water. Pour liquid and meat into the form
and leave it to cool. Before serving, scrape off congealed fat
and turn jelly onto a serving platter.

Ingredients:

- *2 lb. calf's or pig's feet*
- *³/₄ lb. boneless lean pork or veal*
- *¹/₂ lb. soup vegetables (carrot, parsnip, leek and celery root)*
- *1 large onion*
- *1–2 bay leaves*
- *1–2 garlic cloves*
- *a few allspice seeds and peppercorns*
- *salt*
- *ground pepper*

Steak tartare

*R*emove sinew and rinse beef tenderloin.
Grind, add mustard, olive oil, 1 egg yolk, parsley, salt
and pepper to taste. Form it into flattened mounds
on a plate, place fresh egg yolk on top of each mound.
Surround mounds with finely chopped onion,
finely diced pickles and capers. Serve immediately.

Ingredients:

- ³/₄ – 1 lb. beef tenderloin
- 2 egg yolks
- 1 large onion
- 1 T. prepared mustard
- 1 T. olive oil
- 2 small pickles
- 3 T. capers
- 1 t. finely chopped parsley
- salt
- ground pepper to taste

Cooked vegetable salad

*C*ook vegetables in a large quantity of salted water
(you may also use soup vegetables from making bouillon).
Drain and peel boiled potatoes.
Dice vegetables and pickles. Add canned green peas, onion,
pickled mushrooms, and peeled chopped apple
sprinkled with lemon juice. Add mayonnaise and gently mix
(best to use two forks). Add salt, pepper and sugar to taste.
Serve on lettuce leaves, garnish with tomato wedges.

Ingredients:

- *$\frac{1}{2}$ lb. potatoes (boiled with skin)*
- *$\frac{1}{4}$ lb. carrots*
- *$\frac{1}{4}$ lb. celery*
- *$\frac{1}{8}$ lb. parsnip*
- *1 can green peas*
- *$\frac{1}{4}$ lb. pickles*
- *1 large apple (not sweet)*
- *1 t. finely chopped onion*
- *1 t. lemon juice*
- *1 T. finely chopped pickled mushrooms (optional)*

- *1 c. mayonnaise*
- *salt*
- *ground pepper*
- *sugar*

Garnish:
- *lettuce*
- *tomato*

17

Spring salad

*M*ix farmer cheese with sour cream, add washed and sliced radishes, rinsed and finely chopped chives or spring onions, peeled cucumber sliced thin or diced, salt to taste and mix. Serve with wholegrain bread and butter.

Ingredients:

- *³/₄ lb. farmer cheese*
- *1 c. sour cream*
- *20 radishes*
- *1 cucumber*
- *1 small bunch chives or spring onions*
- *salt*

Tripe

*T*horoughly wash tripe, scald with boiling water, scrub,
cut off dark ends, rinse once again, put into boiling water
and cook covered for 15 minutes. Drain, put into freshy
salted boiling water, cover and cook on a low flame
until completely tender (about 4 hours).
Drain, save some stock, cool and cut into thin strips.
Clean, wash and finely chop carrot, celery and parsnip.
Peel all but one onion, slice finely, add to the vegetables,
then add boiling bouillon, add tripe and 1 T. butter, cook about
45 minutes covered. Finely chop the remaining onion,
fry in 1 T. butter until transparent but not browned, add flour,
mix with 2 T. water, bring to a boil, adding a little tripe stock.
Add to tripe, bring to a boil, add salt, pepper and red pepper to taste
if desired. Serve with grated yellow cheese and fresh rolls.

Ingredients:

- 2 lb. beef tripe
- 2 c. rich beef bouillon
- 2 lb. vegetables
  (carrot, celery root,
  parsnip, leek)
- ¾ lb. onion
- 2 T. butter
- 1 T. flour
- salt

- nutmeg
- ground pepper
- hot red pepper
- ginger
- marjoram
- bay leaf
- allspice
- 2 T. grated yellow cheese

Bean soup à la Brètonne

Rinse dry beans and soak overnight in cold water. Cook in the same water, slightly salted, together with bacon, until beans are tender. Peel onion, dice, brown slightly in cooking oil, add flour, make a roux, add some bean stock and tomato paste. Mix and add to beans. Dice Vienna sausage (without wrappers) and bacon, add to bean soup and bring it to a boil. Add salt, a pinch of paprika, and sugar to taste if desired.

Ingredients:

- $3/4$ lb. dry white beans (preferably lima beans)
- $1/4$ lb. slab bacon
- $1/4$ lb. Vienna sausage
- 2 T. cooking oil
- 1 medium onion
- 5–6 T. tomato paste
- 1 T. flour
- salt
- sugar
- paprika

Bigos
(meat & sauerkraut stew)

 inely chop sauerkraut, scald with a small quantity of boiling water and cook together with rinsed mushrooms about 1 hour. Rinse, salt and fry meat together with diced fatback. Add to sauerkraut together with slab bacon, add wine and cook for another 40 minutes until tender. Take out meat, slab bacon and mushrooms and dice them. Remove sausage skin, slice sausage and add to the stew. Gently brown onion until transparent, add flour, mix with 1 T. water and add to the stew. Bring the stew to a boil. Add salt, pepper and sugar to taste.

Note: You may add different kinds of meat to the stew (leftover roast meat, game or poultry).
Bigos is very tasty when reheated.

Ingredients:

- 2–2$\frac{1}{2}$ lb. sauerkraut
- $\frac{1}{2}$ lb. boneless pork
- $\frac{1}{2}$ lb. veal
- $\frac{1}{2}$ lb. sausage
- $\frac{1}{4}$ lb. slab bacon
- $\frac{1}{4}$ oz. dry mushrooms
- 2 oz. fatback
- 1 large onion
- $\frac{1}{2}$ c. red wine (optional)
- 1 T. flour
- salt
- ground pepper
- sugar

Beet sour

*P*eel, rinse and slice beets and cover with pre-boiled lukewarm water in a crockery bowl or a jar. Add a slice of rye bread with the crust, cover the mouth of the jar or bowl with cheesecloth and let stand at room temperature for a few days. Then strain through cheesecloth, pour into a bottle and seal it. Store in a cool place (in the basement or fridge).

Traditional Christmas Eve
barszcz with mushroom-filled *uszka*
(*pierogi* for soup)

*C*lean, wash and cut vegetables. Peel, rinse and slice beets. Add cold salted water (approx. 6 c.). Simmer with 1 t. butter until vegetables are tender. Strain. Add garlic crushed with salt, beet sour, a little mushroom stock (see *uszka* recipe next page), sugar and pepper to taste. Before serving add 1 t. butter to hot soup and sprinkle with finely chopped parsley. Serve hot with *uszka*.

Ingredients:

Beet sour:
- *3–3½ lb. beets*
- *slice of rye bread with the crust*

Traditional Christmas Eve *barszcz*:
- *1 lb. beet*
- *½ lb. soup vegetables (carrot, parsnip, celery root, leek)*
- *2 t. butter*
- *salt*
- *ground pepper*
- *sugar*
- *garlic clove*
- *1–2 c. beet sour*
- *mushroom stock*
- *1 T. finely chopped parsley*

29

Cold barszcz

*R*inse baby beets and their greens, cut into short strips.
Peel and cut beet and cook together with baby beets
in a small amount of water until tender, adding
a pinch of sugar. Just before taking it off the flame,
add citric acid or 1 t. lemon juice. Take out beet.
Mix sour milk with cream, add cooled baby beets
with beet stock, chopped dill, peeled and diced cucumber,
stir and cool.
Serve with quartered hard-boiled eggs.
You may also add diced roast veal.

Ingredients:

- *8 c. sour unpasteurized milk*
- *a few T. thick sour cream*
- *1 bunch baby beets*
- *1 bunch dill*
- *dash of citric acid or 1 t. lemon juice*
- *1 medium beet*
- *1 cucumber*
- *2 hard-boiled eggs*
- *salt*
- *sugar*

Split pea soup with smoked meat

*R*inse split peas and soak in cold water overnight.
Cook in the same water, strain and rub through a sieve.
Cook soup vegetables and bacon in 7 c. salted water to make
a bouillon. Rub the cooked vegetables through a sieve.
Add sieved peas and vegetables to the boullion.
Fry finely chopped onion until light golden, add flour, make a roux,
add a few T. cold water to make a smooth mixture and add it
to the soup. Crush garlic with salt, crush marjoram, add to the soup
and bring it to a boil. Serve hot soup with diced bacon.
You may also add butter-fried white bread croutons.

Ingredients:

- *$3/4$ lb. split peas*
- *$1/2$ lb. soup vegetables (carrot, parsnip, celery root, leek)*
- *$1/4$ lb. slab bacon*
- *1 onion*
- *1 T. butter*
- *1 rounded T. flour*
- *1–2 garlic cloves*
- *marjoram*
- *salt*

Sauerkraut soup

Clean and rinse vegetables. Put them in 7 c. cold salted water,
add a bay leaf and bring to a boil.
Drain sauerkraut and set the sauerkraut juice aside.
Finely chop sauerkraut, cover with boiling strained bouillon,
add bacon and bring to a boil. Fry finely chopped onion together
with finely diced fatback until the onion is light golden.
Add separately browned flour, mix with a small quantity of water,
add to the bouillon and bring to a boil. Take the bacon out,
dice and put back in the soup. Add sauerkraut juice,
and pepper and salt to taste.

Ingredients:

- $3/4$ –1 lb. sauerkraut
- $1/4$ lb. slab bacon
- $1/2$ lb. soup vegetables
  (carrot, parsnip,
  celery root, leek)
- 2 oz. fatback
- 1 onion
- 3 T. flour
- salt
- ground pepper
- bay leaf

Barley soup

*R*inse barley groats, cover with cold water (2 c.),
add 1 t. butter, simmer on low heat until tender (about 15 minutes).
Soak mushrooms for a few hours and cook mushrooms, cleaned
vegetables and giblets in 7 c. water. Strain the bouillon.
Cut mushrooms and vegetables into strips. Cook peeled and diced
potatoes in the bouillon. Combine the bouillon with the barley,
mushrooms and vegetables, and salt to taste. Before serving,
add 1 t. butter and parsley.

Ingredients:

- *1/2 lb. soup vegetables
  (carrot, parsnip,
  celery root, leek)*
- *chicken wings, neck
  and hearts*
- *2–3 dried mushrooms*
- *$^{1}/_{2}$ c. barley groats*
- *4–5 medium-sized
  potatoes*
- *2 t. butter*
- *1 t. chopped parsley*
- *salt*

Mushroom soup
with square noodles (*łazanki*)

*C*over well-rinsed mushrooms with cold water for 2 hours. Cook in the same water until tender, adding chopped onion. Clean and wash vegetables, cook in 7 c. salted water. Drain and combine the bouillon with drained mushroom stock. Brown the flour in cooking oil until it is a light-golden roux, add a few T. cold water. Add the roux to the bouillon with mushroom stock and bring to a boil. Add sour cream mixed with a small quantity of soup, add salt and pepper to taste and mushrooms cut into strips. Sprinkle with parsley. Serve with square noodles prepared in advance.

Square noodles: Sift flour onto a breadboard, break 1 egg on top of it, add salt and knead into dough, gradually adding lukewarm water. The resulting dough should be rather firm. Roll out thin and let dry. Sprinkle with flour, roll up into a wide roll. Cut the roll into $^1/_2$-inch strips. Pile up a few strips and cut them into squares. Scatter over a floured board and let dry for a while. Drop into salted boiling water, stir, cook, drain, add 1 t. cooking oil.

Ingredients:

Soup:
- $^1/_2$ lb. soup vegetables (carrot, parsnip, celery root, leek)
- $1^1/_2$ oz. dried mushrooms
- 3 T. flour
- 2 T. cooking oil
- $^1/_2$ c. sour cream
- 1 t. finely chopped parsley
- salt
- pepper

Łazanki:
- $^3/_4$ c. flour
- 1 egg
- salt
- 1 t. cooking oil

Ryemeal soup (*żurek*) with sausage

*C*ook a bouillon from soup vegetables and 6 c. water.
Shortly before straining, add the sausage.
Peel potatoes, cut into large cubes and cook in boiling,
lightly salted bouillon. Mix flour with a few T. water,
add to the bouillon along with ryemeal sour, sliced sausage,
and garlic crushed with salt, and bring the soup to a boil.

Ingredients:

Ryemeal sour:
- *mix $^3/_4$ c. rye flour with 2 c. pre-boiled warm water. Pour into a jar or crockery bowl, cover with cheesecloth and let stand in a warm place for 4–5 days.*

Żurek:
- *$^1/_2$ lb. soup vegetables (carrot, parsnip, celery root, leek)*
- *$^1/_2$ lb. sausage*
- *1 lb. potatoes*
- *2 c. ryemeal sour*
- *1 rounded T. flour*
- *garlic clove*
- *salt*

Veal in paprika sauce with egg-batter dumplings

*R*inse the meat and pat dry, cut into small pieces, salt, sprinkle with pepper and part of the flour, then fry all sides in cooking oil briefly and place in a pot. Add butter, peeled and finely chopped onion and garlic crushed with salt, add $\frac{1}{2}$ c. water and stew on a low flame for 40–45 minutes, adding more water as the sauce evaporates. When the meat is tender, add paprika, sprinkle and stir in the remaining flour and bring to a boil, then add sour cream. Serve with egg-batter dumplings.

Dumplings: Break 1 egg onto sifted flour in a bowl, add salt, mix and gradually add water, kneading the dough with a wooden spoon. There should be just as much water as needed to work the dough with a spoon – the longer the kneading, the more spongy the dumplings will become. When bubbles begin to form in the dough, take the dough with a metal spoon and drop small, oval dumplings into boiling salted water. Cook covered for a while, then take out using a slotted spoon. Dumplings can be topped with some melted butter.

Ingredients:

Veal in paprika sauce:
- *1–1½ lb. boneless veal (shoulder or neck)*
- *2 T. cooking oil*
- *2 T. flour*
- *1 t. butter*
- *1 large onion*
- *garlic clove*
- *½ c. sour cream*
- *salt*
- *ground pepper*
- *paprika*

Egg-batter dumplings:
- *1 c. flour*
- *1 egg*
- *salt*
- *1 t. butter (optional)*

Polish style veal brisket

*C*arefully rinse the veal brisket, pat dry, place flat on a cutting board and cut where the meat divides into two parts, then widen the "pocket" with your hand. Salt inside and out. For stuffing, soak rolls in milk (do not squeeze out the milk). Grind.
Cream butter or margarine with egg yolks, add soaked rolls, chopped parsley (and dill if desired); add pepper, salt and nutmeg to taste. Then gently mix with egg whites beaten into a stiff froth, adding 1 T. bread crumbs. The stuffing should be rather thick.
If it is not, then add more bread crumbs.
Stuff the "pocket", skewer it closed, place in a roasting pan on butter and sprinkle with water. Roast in a hot oven (390°) for $1-1\frac{1}{2}$ hours, basting with the meat sauce and more water as the sauce evaporates.
Cut nicely browned veal brisket along the ribs.
Serve with boiled potatoes, and a cucumber salad or green salad.

Ingredients:

- *2 lb. veal brisket*
- *1 T. butter*

Stuffing:
- *2 stale rolls*
- *2 eggs*
- *1/2 c. milk*
- *2 T. butter or margarine*
- *1 T. finely chopped parsley*
- *1 T. chopped dill (optional)*
- *1 T. bread crumbs*
- *ground pepper*
- *salt*
- *a pinch of grated nutmeg*

Roast veal

inse the meat, pat it dry, rub with garlic crushed with salt.
If the meat is flat enough, roll it up and tie with cotton thread.
Heat the cooking oil in a frying pan and brown the meat on all
sides, then place it in a roasting pan, add water and butter and roast
for about 1 hour in a hot oven (390°), adding more water as the
sauce evaporates. Slice across the grain of the meat.
(If the piece of meat is rather small it can be placed
in a pot after frying and then stewed covered with butter
and a small quantity of water until tender.)
Serve with dumplings or boiled potatoes, and salads.

Ingredients:

• *2 lb. boneless veal
(shoulder or rump)*
• *2–3 T. cooking oil*
• *1 T. butter*
• *garlic clove*
• *salt*

Veal cutlets
with carrots and green peas

inse the meat and pat it dry, slice across the grain into four thick slices, then pound lightly until $^1/_2$-inch thick, forming nice cutlets. Salt them on both sides, dredge separately in flour, beaten egg, and then bread crumbs; press the crumbs in so they stick. Fry both sides in cooking oil until golden. When almost fried, add butter and 1 T. water and fry a little while on a low flame. Place a slice of lemon on each cutlet. Serve with boiled potatoes, peas and carrots.

Peas and carrots: Clean, peel and wash the carrots, then dice small, cover with a small amount of boiling, slightly salted and sweetened water and half of the butter. If fresh or frozen peas are used they should be added to the carrots at that point and simmered on a low flame. If canned peas are used, add when the carrots are tender. Take vegetables off the flame, sprinkle with flour, stir and cook again. Just before serving add the remaining butter without cooking.

Ingredients:

Veal cutlets:
- 1$^1/_2$ lb. boneless veal
- 2–3 T. cooking oil
- 1 T. butter
- 1 egg
- 2 T. flour
- 4–5 T. bread crumbs
- 4 lemon slices

Vegetables:
- 1 lb. carrots
- 1/2 lb. green peas (fresh, frozen or canned)
- 1 flat T. flour
- 1 T. butter
- salt
- sugar

Roast lamb

*R*inse the meat, pat it dry and cover with cool marinade
made from 3 c. water boiled with spices and onion slices,
and vinegar added when cooled. Keep the meat and marinade
in a covered pot and let it stand in a cool place for 2 days.
Then take the meat out of the marinade, pat it dry, rub with salt and
garlic, sprinkle with flour, fry in very hot cooking oil
in a frying pan, place in a roasting pan and add more cooking oil.
Roast in a hot oven (390°) for 45–50 minutes,
sprinkling the meat with the leftover marinade
from time to time.

Ingredients:

- *2 lb. lamb (with bones)*
- *2 T. flour*
- *garlic clove*
- *salt*
- *cooking oil*

Marinade:
- *1 c. vinegar*
- *a few peppercorns*
- *a few allspice seeds*
- *2 t. salt*
- *1 medium onion*

57

Pot roast with beets

*R*inse the meat, pat it dry, remove the gristle, lightly pound, insert sticks of salted fatback, then salt and sprinkle with flour. Heat cooking oil in a frying pan and brown the meat on all sides, then place it in a pot, add onion slices, the remaining oil and 2–3 T. water; simmer on a low flame until the onion is transparent. Add $\frac{1}{2}$ c. water, 1 t. seasoned salt and stew for about 2 hours on a low flame until tender, adding water from time to time. When the meat is tender, add the remaining flour to the sauce and cook. Serve the pot roast cut in thin slices across the grain and topped with the sauce, and with boiled potatoes and beets.

Beets: Scrub the beets with a brush, rinse and cook in boiling water until tender or else bake in an oven. Peel and grate them thick, add salt and sugar and stir in flour mixed with a few T. water. Boil, add sour cream, lemon juice or citric acid, and sugar to taste.

Ingredients:

Pot roast:
- *$1\frac{1}{2}$ lb. boneless beef (best is rump or chuck)*
- *3 T. cooking oil*
- *2 oz. fatback*
- *2 large onions*
- *2 T. flour*
- *1 t. seasoned salt*
- *salt*

Beets:
- *$1\frac{1}{2}$ lb. beets*
- *1 T. flour*
- *$\frac{1}{2}$ c. sour cream*
- *salt*
- *sugar*
- *lemon juice or citric acid*

Boiled beef in horseradish sauce

Rinse the meat, put into salted boiling water and cook on a low flame. Clean and wash soup vegetables and add them to the cooking meat. Carefully wash unpeeled onion, halve it and brown over a flame, add it to the meat when it becomes tender, along with cleaned and rinsed cabbage.
Cut the meat into slices across the grain. Serve with horseradish sauce, and with the vegetables taken from the bouillon if desired.

Sauce: Finely grate peeled and rinsed horseradish, add lemon juice and sugar. Mix the flour with cooled bouillon, boil, add grated horseradish, salt and sugar to taste. Bring to a boil, take off the flame and add thick sour cream. Do not boil again.

Ingredients:

- 1 ¹⁄₂ lb. boneless veal (chuck or rump)
- ¹⁄₂ lb. cabbage
- ¹⁄₂ lb. soup vegetables (carrot, parsnip, celery root, leek)
- 1 large onion
- salt
- a few peppercorns

Sauce:
- ¹⁄₄ lb. horseradish
- 1–1¹⁄₂ T. flour
- 1 c. meat bouillon
- ¹⁄₂ c. sour cream
- salt
- sugar
- lemon juice or citric acid

Pork cutlets with cabbage

inse the pork, pat it dry, cut into equal steaks, score them a few times, gently pound, salt; dredge in flour, then in egg beaten with a fork, then in bread crumbs. Form nice oval cutlets, pat the bread crumbs in so they stick. Fry both sides in pre-heated cooking oil until light golden, then add $\frac{1}{2}$ T. water and simmer covered on a low flame for a while. Before serving take off the cover and cook off the water. Serve with cooked cabbage.

Cooked cabbage: Discard outer leaves, carefully wash and finely chop. Add 1 c. salted boiling water and cook covered. Uncover, simmer a few minutes on a low flame and cover again. When almost tender, add peeled and chopped apples and caraway and continue to cook on a low flame. Finely chop peeled onion, fry in cooking oil until golden, add flour and mix it with the oil and then add a few T. water. Cook this mixture, add to cooked cabbage and stir. Cook all together, add salt, sugar and citric acid (optional) to taste.

Ingredients:

Pork cutlets:
- *1 $\frac{1}{2}$ lb. boneless pork*
- *2 T. cooking oil*
- *2 T. flour*
- *1 egg*
- *4–5 T. bread crumbs*

Cooked cabbage:
- *2 lb. cabbage*
- *3–4 apples (not sweet)*
- *2 medium onions*
- *2 T. flour*
- *2 T. cooking oil*
- *1 t. caraway seeds*
- *salt*
- *sugar*
- *citric acid (optional)*

Meatballs with barley groats

Rinse the meat and pat it dry. Soak the roll in milk, squeeze out the milk and grind the meat and the rool. Add 1 egg, garlic and finely chopped onion browned in cooking oil until transparent, add pepper and salt and mix well. Form small meatballs with moistened hands, dredge in flour and fry all sides in pre-heated cooking oil. When slightly browned, add ¹/₂ c. water, cover and stew on a low flame for 20–25 minutes, supplementing the water when needed. Serve with barley (or buckwheat) groats and sauerkraut salad.

Groats: Clean the groats, rinse and let dry in a strainer. When completely dry, sprinkle with cooking oil, drop into 2 c. boiling salted water, stir and bring to a boil quickly in the top of a double boiler directly on the burner. Cover. When groats have absorbed the water completely, fit that pot into the bottom pot with boiling water and cook on a low flame until tender.

Ingredients:

Meatballs:
- ¹/₂ lb. beef
- ¹/₂ lb. pork
- 1 stale roll
- 1 egg
- 1 medium onion
- ¹/₂ c. milk
- 2–3 T. flour
- 2–3 T. cooking oil
- ground pepper
- salt
- garlic clove (optional)

Barley groats:
- 1 c. barley
- 1¹/₂ T. cooking oil
- salt

Roll-ups in bread with buckwheat groats

Rinse the meat, pat it dry, cut across the grain into four slices, pound and sprinkle with salt and pepper. Peel the onion, slice it and brown in 1 T. cooking oil until transparent, then arrange the slices on the meat fillets and cover with slices of bacon. Roll up the meat, dredge in flour, skewer, and brown on all sides in cooking oil. Place the meat in a pan, add a few T. water and the butter, and stew on a low flame for 40–45 minutes until tender. Cut off the top of the bread, hollow it, put the roll-ups with the sauce inside, top with sour cream, cover with the top of the bread and bake in the oven at 360–390° for half an hour. Serve the meat in the bread, and buckwheat groats and pickles on the side.

Groats: Clean the buckwheat groats, sprinkle with cooking oil and drop into 2 c. salted boiling water in the top half of a double boiler directly on the burner. Stir and bring to a boil quickly, then cover. When the buckwheat groats have absorbed the water completely, fit the pot into the bottom pot with boiling water and cook on a low flame until tender.

Ingredients:

Roll-ups in bread:
- *1½ lb. boneless beef*
- *1 large onion*
- *4 slices bacon*
- *2–3 T. flour*
- *3–4 T. cooking oil*
- *1 T. butter*
- *ground pepper*
- *salt*
- *½ c. sour cream*
- *1 loaf of wholegrain bread*

Buckwheat groats:
- *1 c. buckwheat groats*
- *1–1½ T. cooking oil*
- *salt*

"Swallow nests"

ound meat into large fillets, salt and pepper both sides
and then sprinkle generously with parsley.
Place a piece of ham and a shelled hard-boiled egg on each fillet.
Roll up and tie with white thread, dredge in flour and quick-fry
in pre-heated cooking oil. Transfer to a pot, add butter and some
water, and stew covered for 30–35 minutes,
supplementing water if needed.
Before serving remove the thread.
Cut each roll-up into halves across the egg.
Serve in the sauce with boiled or mashed potatoes.

Ingredients:

- *4 large veal fillets cut across the grain (2 lb.)*
- *4 eggs*
- *3 T. finely chopped parsley*
- *4 slices fat ham*
- *2 T. flour*
- *2–3 T. cooking oil*
- *1 T. butter*
- *salt*
- *ground pepper*

Poultry

Fried chicken Polonaise
with Polish cucumber salad 73

Turkey stuffed with raisins and almonds 74

Stuffed chicken 75

Turkey steaks 77

Duck with apples 79

Fried chicken Polonaise with Polish cucumber salad

*R*inse chicken, then quarter, salt and dredge in flour, then beaten egg and then bread crumbs. Fry on a high flame until golden, add 2–3 T. water and cook covered on a low flame until tender. Just before serving, uncover (you may add a bit of butter) and brown until skin is crispy. Serve with new potatoes and Polish cucumber salad.

Salad: Peel cucumbers, slice very thin, add sour cream mixed with salt, sugar, and vinegar (if desired). Sprinkle with chopped dill.

Ingredients:

Chickens:
- *2 small chickens*
- *5–6 T. bread crumbs*
- *3–4 T. flour*
- *1 egg*
- *salt*
- *4–5 T. cooking oil or margarine*
- *1 t. butter (optional)*

Cucumber salad:
- *1 lb. fresh cucumber*
- *1 T. finely chopped dill*
- *salt*
- *sugar*
- *1 t. wine vinegar (optional)*
- *$\frac{1}{2}$ c. sour cream*

Turkey steaks

*C*ut turkey breast into steaks across the grain,
pound gently to tenderize, form oval cutlets, salt, dredge in flour
and then beaten egg. Cut stale roll into small sticks,
add to bread crumbs. Dredge cutlets on both sides in bread
crumbs and croutons, fry in pre-heated oil until light golden,
then add butter and fry or bake a little more on low heat.
Serve with boiled potatoes and green salad.

Ingredients:

- *$1\frac{1}{2}$ lb. turkey breast*
- *2–3 T. flour*
- *1 egg*
- *2–3 T. bread crumbs*
- *1 stale roll*
  (without crust)
- *3 T. cooking oil*
- *3 T. oz. butter*
- *salt*

Duck with apples

*R*inse the duck, rub inside and out with salt, pepper and marjoram. Put parsley inside. Place duck in a roasting pan, add a little butter and roast in a hot oven (480°) until nicely browned. When almost tender, pour in half of the calvados and cover tightly with aluminum foil so the duck will absorb the calvados. Peel, core and quarter the apples, then sprinkle with pepper and fry in the remaining butter. Add half-tender apples to the duck, sprinkle with the rest of the calvados and roast a little longer. Serve with boiled or roasted potatoes.

Ingredients:

- *1 young duck*
- *2–2$\frac{1}{2}$ lb. apples (green, not sweet)*
- *$\frac{1}{2}$ c. calvados*
- *2 rounded T. butter*
- *a small bunch of parsley*
- *salt*
- *ground pepper*
- *marjoram*

79

Fish entrées

Carp in grey sauce 83

Fried carp 85

Poached trout 87

Walleye baked in sour cream 89

Eel in dill sauce 91

Carp in grey sauce

cale the carp and rinse outside surface,
then carefully gut it, being careful not to spill the gall.
Do not rinse inside. Cut into $1\frac{1}{2}$-inch steaks and salt them.
Put peeled and diced celery root and sliced onion
into beer diluted with 1 pt. water, add spices
and a piece of lemon peel and boil until vegetables are soft
(about 20 minutes). Then put in the carp sprinkled with lemon juice,
and simmer on a low flame about 15–20 minutes.
Take the fish out carefully and put it on a platter (keep warm).
Rub the remaining fish stock through a sieve (removing pepper
and allspice), add finely crumbled honey cake, plum jam, raisins
and slivered almonds. Boil the sauce, add sugar to taste.
Cover carp with sauce. Serve the rest of the sauce in a gravy boat.
Goes well with fine buckwheat groats (*kasza krakowska*)
or with boiled potatoes.

Ingredients:

- *carp (2 lb.)*
- *lemon*
- *celery root ($\frac{1}{4}$ lb.)*
- *onion ($\frac{1}{4}$ lb.)*
- *1 pt. beer*
- *2 T. butter*
- *1 T. plum jam*
- *$\frac{1}{4}$ lb. dried honey cake (optional)*
- *$\frac{1}{4}$ lb. light raisins*
- *$\frac{1}{4}$ lb. dark raisins*
- *$\frac{1}{4}$ lb. slivered almonds*
- *5–6 peppercorns*
- *5–6 allspice seeds*
- *a pinch of ginger*
- *salt*
- *sugar*

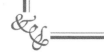

Fried carp

*R*inse and pat dry carp steaks. Sprinkle with salt
and pepper. Beat 1 egg on a flat dish using a fork.
Dredge the steaks in flour, then in egg and then bread crumbs.
Pat the steaks to fix the bread crumbs. Fry until light golden.
After frying place in a hot oven or simmer covered on a low flame
for a few minutes to make sure that the fish is well cooked inside.
Serve with mashed potatoes and horseradish.

Prepared horseradish: Grate horseradish,
season with lemon juice and sugar, add rich sour cream.
Sour cream may be replaced with whipped fresh cream
(horseradish prepared in this way is very light).
Carp steaks may be fried without egg and bread crumbs,
dredged in flour only.

Ingredients:

- *2 lb. carp steaks*
- *1 egg*
- *2 T. flour*
- *5–6 T. bread crumbs*
- *3 T. cooking oil
  or butter*
- *salt*
- *ground pepper*

Poached trout

Clean the vegetables. Boil a bouillon of vegetables,
spices and 2 pt. water. Strain and salt the bouillon.
Gut and rinse trout, leaving heads attached.
Arrange the trout in a fish pot and pour in hot bouillon.
Simmer on a low flame for about 15 minutes.
Place the fish on a serving platter and pour melted butter
over them, garnish with egg slices, parsley and lemon slices.

Ingredients:

• *4 rainbow trout
(approx. $\frac{1}{2}$ lb. each)*
• *$\frac{1}{2}$ lb. vegetables (carrots,
celery root, parsnips, leek)*
• *1 small onion*
• *4–5 allspice seeds*
• *1–2 bay leaves*
• *2 T. butter*
• *2 hard-boiled eggs*
• *parsley and lemon slices
for decoration*

Walleye baked in sour cream

*R*inse the steaks, sprinkle with salt,
dredge in flour and quick-fry in a frying pan until golden.
Transfer to a fire-proof platter, sprinkling with wine and melted
cooking oil (or butter). Bake covered for about 30 minutes,
sprinkling with a little water while baking.
When almost baked, pour on sour cream.

Ingredients:

- *1 1/2 lb. walleye steaks*
- *1 rounded T. flour*
- *3 T. cooking oil or butter*
- *1/2 glass white wine*
- *1/2 c. sour cream*
- *salt*

Eel in dill sauce

*G*ut, remove skin, rinse and salt the eel. Pour 3 pt. cold water
into a pot with cleaned and rinsed soup vegetables,
halved onion, bay leaf and allspice. Boil about half an hour.
Put the fish into the boiling bouillon and simmer
another 30–35 minutes on a low flame. Take the eel out,
place it on a serving platter and pour hot dill sauce on it.
Serve with boiled potatoes.

Dill sauce: Strain the bouillon (approx. 1 pint).
Mix the flour with a few t. water, combine with the fish bouillon
and boil, then add dill, sour cream and butter.

Ingredients:

- *2 lb. eel*
- *½ lb. soup vegetables (carrot, parsnip, celery root, leek)*
- *1 onion*
- *bay leaf*
- *4–5 allspice seeds*
- *3–4 T. finely chopped dill*
- *3 T. flour*
- *½ c. sour cream*
- *1 t. butter*
- *salt*

Cabbage rolls (gołąbki) with tomato sauce

*B*oil rice until not quite tender, strain and add onion browned
in cooking oil and ground pork. Add salt and pepper to taste.
Place the entire cabbage (after removing the core)
into a large quantity of boiling water. Carefully separate each leaf
and put once again into the boiling water, a few at a time.
Cook briefly, then remove with a slotted spoon and let drain.
When cooled, cut out the thick part of the main vein, center
the rice-and-meat filling on the leaves, fold the edges in and roll tight.
Arrange *gołąbki* on cooked cabbage leaves placed on the bottom of the
pot (in 2–3 layers), cover with the remaining leaves, add a cup of
boiling salted water, and cook on a low flame for about 45 minutes,
or else stew in the oven in a casserole, also on low heat (about 250°).
When tender, discard the leaves from the top.
Serve with hot tomato sauce.

Sauce: Brown finely minced onion in butter until transparent,
add flour, mix, add in cold bouillon and then tomato paste.
Cook on a low flame. Add salt and sugar to taste.

Ingredients:

Cabbage rolls (*gołąbki*):
- *1 cabbage
(not very compact,
approx. 3 lb.)*
- *¹/₂ lb. ground pork*
- *1 c. rice*
- *1 onion*
- *3 T. cooking oil*
- *salt*
- *ground pepper*

Tomato sauce:
- *2 T. tomato paste*
- *2 T. flour*
- *1 T. butter*
- *¹/₂ c. sour cream*
- *1 small onion*
- *1 c. bouillon*
- *salt*
- *pepper*
- *sugar*

Egg croquettes

*B*oil eggs hard (8–10 minutes), cover with cold water.
Halve with a sharp knife, remove eggs from the shells,
being careful not to crush the shells. Chop the eggs, add parsley
and finely chopped onion or chives, season with salt and pepper
and mix. Fill the eggshells with egg mix, lightly pressing with
a spoon. When all shells are filled and there is no egg mix left,
turn out the shells on a plate sprinkled with bread crumbs
so that the molds stick to the bread crumbs flat side down.
Fry in cooking oil for a few minutes on a medium flame,
preferably covered. Serve with fried potatoes and green salad.

Ingredients:

- *8 eggs*
- *1 medium onion
or a bunch of chives*
- *2 T. finely chopped
parsley*
- *2–3 T. bread crumbs*
- *salt*
- *ground pepper*
- *4 T. cooking oil*

"Vegetable bouquet"

*P*lace the cauliflower in salted, slightly sweetened boiling water, and cook until tender.
Place cleaned asparagus shoots standing up in a high narrow pot, add salted, slightly sweetened boiling water, so that the tops stick out of the water. Cover and cook for 15–20 minutes.
Clean carrots, cut into sticks, cook in salted, slightly sweetened water and 1 t. butter until tender.
Cook the peas in a small quantity of salted boiling water until tender, then sprinkle with flour, cook a little longer and add 1 t. butter.
Just before the vegetables are done, brown bread crumbs until golden on a dry frying pan and add melted butter.
Arrange a "bouquet" of vegetables on each plate and pour the roux over the cauliflower and asparagus shoots.

Ingredients:

- *1 cauliflower*
- *$\frac{1}{2}$ lb. asparagus shoots*
- *$\frac{1}{2}$ lb. young carrots*
- *$\frac{1}{2}$ lb. green peas*
- *3 T. butter*
- *1 t. flour*
- *3 T. bread crumbs*
- *salt*
- *sugar*

Russian-style *pierogi*

*C*lean potatoes with a brush, cook, peel and grind
together with farmer cheese. Finely chop onion and brown
in cooking oil until golden, add to potato-and-cheese mixture,
add salt and pepper, then mix completely.
Sift the flour onto a breadboard, break 1 egg on it, add salt
and approx. 1 cup lukewarm water. Knead the dough well,
not very firm. Divide into parts. Roll out one part thin;
cover the other parts with a bowl to protect from drying.
Cut 2-inch circles from the rolled-out dough sheet using a glass or
cookie cutter. Spoon the filling into the middle of each circle, fold
dough in half and pinch the edges together.

Place the *pierogi* on a tray sprinkled with flour and cover with
cheesecloth. Boil water in a wide, low kettle, add salt, and drop in
the dumplings a few at a time. Cover, and when they rise to the
surface, uncover and keep on a low flame a little longer. They will
fall apart if cooked too long. Take out using a slotted spoon and
sprinkle with onion browned in butter, or else fried diced fatback.

Ingredients:

Dough:
- 2–2½ c. flour
- 1 egg
- salt

Topping:
- 2 T. butter or margarine
- 1 onion or 2 oz. fatback

Filling:
- 2 lb. potatoes
- ½ lb. farmer cheese
- 1 onion
- 2 T. cooking oil
- salt
- ground pepper

Kopytka
(potato dumplings)

Boil peeled potatoes in salted water, drain, mash with milk,
1 rounded t. butter and a pinch of salt, then leave to cool.
When cool, grind, place on a breadboard, break 1 egg and sift some
flour on it. Knead the dough quickly, adding the remaining flour
a little at a time. Boil water in a large wide pot, so that the *kopytka*
can be dropped immediately into hot water as soon as they are cut,
because the dough soon gets damp.
Form long fingers of dough, flatten slightly and cut at an angle into
bite-size pieces. Put them in boiling salted water a few at a time.
When they rise to the surface, take out with a slotted spoon
and place in a large bowl, adding some butter to each portion
so they do not stick together, and gently shake the bowl.
Keep covered until all *kopytka* are cooked.
Serve with meat and sauce or as a separate dish with mushroom
or tomato sauce. They are also tasty fried in cooking oil.

Ingredients:

- $2\frac{1}{4}$ lb. potatoes
- $1\frac{3}{4}$ c. flour
- 1 egg
- 1 rounded T. butter
- 3 T. milk
- salt

Potato croquettes
with mushroom sauce

*B*rush and rinse potatoes, cook whole and unpeeled, leave to cool and then peel them. Grind, add eggs, flour, and chopped onion browned in cooking oil. Add salt and pepper to taste and mix into a smooth mass. Form the mass into a thick roll on a breadboard, cut into pieces and form oval, medium-size croquettes, dredge in bread crumbs and fry both sides in hot cooking oil until golden.
Serve with mushroom sauce.

Sauce: soak carefully cleaned mushrooms in cold water for a few hours. Cook in the same water, save the liquid and chop the mushrooms. Fry finely minced onion in cooking oil until transparent, mix with chopped mushrooms, sprinkle with flour, add cold mushroom liquid and cook, then mix in sour cream and add salt and pepper to taste.

Ingredients:

Potato croquettes:
- $2^{1}/_{2}$ lb. potatoes
- 1 T. cooking oil
- 1 onion
- 2 eggs
- 5 T. flour
- 1 T. finely chopped parsley
- 2–3 T. bread crumbs
- 3–4 T. cooking oil
- salt
- ground pepper

Sauce:
- 1 oz. dried mushrooms
- 1 small onion
- 3 T. cooking oil
- 3 T. flour
- $^{1}/_{2}$ c. sour cream
- salt
- ground pepper

107

Potato pancakes

*P*eel and rinse potatoes, finely grate, then lightly press out
some of the water. Add grated onion, 1 egg, flour, salt and pepper
and mix. Heat cooking oil or lard in a frying pan until very hot,
fry flattened dollops of potato mixture quickly on both sides.
Best if served right from the frying pan, with sour cream.
May be served with coleslaw or mushroom sauce.
If you wish to serve the pancakes with sugar or jam,
omit onion and pepper.

Ingredients:

- *3 lb. potatoes*
- *1 onion*
- *1 egg*
- *2 T. flour*
- *salt*
- *ground pepper*
- *cooking oil for frying*

Pierogi leniwe
("lazy pierogi")

Grind farmer cheese into a bowl, then add egg yolks and salt.
Beat egg whites into a stiff froth and stir in alternately
with the cheese and sifted flour, then mix. Turn out the pastry
on a breadboard, form 1-inch-thick rolls, slightly flatten, cross-hatch
with the dull side of a knife, then cut at an angle into bite-size
pieces and drop into boiling, salted water.
When they rise to the surface, take out with a slotted spoon.
Serve with melted butter with browned bread crumbs.

Ingredients:

• 1½ lb. farmer cheese
• 2–3 eggs
• 1½ c. flour
• salt
• 1 T. bread crumbs
• 1 T. butter

Sauerkraut and mushroom crepes

*B*reak the eggs into sifted flour, add cooking oil and salt, pour in milk and mix in a blender until the batter is smooth. Add water gradually, depending on how thick the batter is. Cover the batter with a towel and leave for 30–60 minutes. Then fry crepes on a non-stick frying pan (or a regular frying pan greased with a piece of fatback). Crepes should spread over the entire surface of the frying pan. Fill the ready crepes and roll them up, then dredge the rolled crepes in beaten egg and then bread crumbs. Just before serving, quick-fry both sides in hot cooking oil.

Filling: Rinse dried mushrooms, soak in a small quantity of cold water for a few hours and cook in the same water until tender. Save the liquid.
Press sour liquid out of the sauerkraut, add mushroom stock and cook covered on low heat. When tender, cook off excess liquid, add mushrooms cut into thin strips, finely chopped onion (first browned in cooking oil until transparent), and add salt and pepper to taste. Sprinkle with flour and cook a little longer.

Ingredients:

Batter:
- *2 eggs*
- *1 ½ c. flour*
- *1 T. cooking oil*
- *1 c. milk*
- *½ c. water*
- *salt*
- *a piece of fatback to grease frying pan (optional)*

Filling:
- *1 lb. sauerkraut*
- *2 oz. dried mushrooms*
- *1 large onion*
- *1 T. flour*
- *2 T. cooking oil*
- *salt*
- *ground pepper*

For frying ready crepes:
- *1 egg*
- *bread crumbs*
- *cooking oil*

Cheese crepes

Grind the cheese, add powdered sugar, vanilla sugar
and egg yolks, and mix into a smooth mass,
then add raisins and orange peel.
Spread the mixture on the crepes, roll up or fold into triangles.
Serve after frying lightly. Sprinkle with powdered sugar.
Top with sour cream if desired.
Many people like them best with cherry preserves.

Ingredients:

Batter:
*as for sauerkraut and
mushroom crepes*

Filling:
- *1 lb. farmer cheese*
- *2 egg yolks*
- *3 T. sugar*
- *2–3 T. raisins*
- *1 T. finely chopped
candied orange peel*
- *vanilla sugar*
- *powdered sugar
to sprinkle*
- *sour cream (optional)*

115

Apple fritters (*racuszki*)

Add egg yolks, a pinch of salt and 1 T. olive oil to sifted
flour. Pour milk in, still mixing. Mix the batter in a blender
and leave for 15 minutes covered with a towel.
Peel and core apples and cut into $\frac{1}{4}$-inch slices.
Whisk egg whites into a stiff froth, gently mix with the batter,
which should be smooth like thick cream.
Dip apple slices in the dough, put in hot cooking oil
and fry on a moderate flame until light golden on both sides.
Sprinkle with vanilla sugar and powdered sugar immediately
after removing from the frying pan. Serve hot.

Ingredients:

• *1 lb. apples (not sweet)*
• *1 c. flour*
• *2 eggs*
• *1 T. olive oil*
• *$\frac{3}{4}$ c. milk*
• *salt*
• *cooking oil*
• *powdered sugar and
vanilla sugar to sprinkle*

Plum-filled potato dumplings
(knedle)

Rinse plums and remove pits. Dry the plums in a strainer. Peel, boil and drain potatoes, add 1 t. butter and grind or mash. Break the egg into the potato mass when cooled, add salt, sifted flour and potato starch, quickly knead dough smooth. Form a thick dough roll and cut piece by piece. Pat each piece flat in flour-dusted hands. Roll a plum in each piece and place it on a floured board. Put a few at a time into boiling salted water. When they rise to the surface they are ready. Remove using a slotted spoon. Serve with melted butter or topped with sour cream and sprinkle with powdered sugar.

Ingredients:

- *2 lb. potatoes*
- *1 $\frac{1}{2}$ c. flour*
- *1 T. potato starch*
- *1 egg*
- *1 T. butter*
- *salt*
- *1 $\frac{1}{2}$ lb. plums*
- *sugar to sprinkle*
- *sour cream to top (optional)*

Yeast-raised *babka*

*M*ix the yeast with 1 t. sugar and a few T. warm milk,
cover with a towel and leave in a warm place to grow.
Add salt to dry sifted flower, pour in the yeast and the rest of
the lukewarm milk, gently mix and leave for a few minutes.
When it has risen, add egg yolks mixed with sugar and grated lemon
peel and mix in a blender until smooth (about 10 minutes).
Still mixing, gradually add melted, still-warm butter, then add orange
peel and raisins. When the dough has completely absorbed the butter,
cover it with a towel and leave in a warm place for about
1 hour. When it doubles in volume, put it in a tall hollow-centered cake
form, greased with butter and sprinkled with bread crumbs.
The form should be filled a bit less than
half of its height. Cover the pan with a towel. When the dough has
almost filled the form, brush the top with an egg mixed with
1 t. milk and put into a moderate oven. Bake for about 40–45 minutes at 360°.
When cooled, remove from the form and glaze.

Glaze: Mix powdered sugar with lemon juice and hot water.

Note: The above amount is enough to make 2 *babkas*:
1 large (about 10 inches in diameter) and 1 small
(about 7 inches in diameter).

Ingredients:

Dough:
- *1 lb. wheat flour*
- *1 c. sugar*
- *³⁄₄ c. butter or margarine*
- *5 egg yolks*
- *1 c. milk*
- *2 oz. yeast*
- *½ flat t. salt*
- *2 oz. raisins*

- *1 T. finely chopped candied orange peel, grated lemon peel (scalded with hot water)*
- *1 egg to brush the* babka
- *butter and bread crumbs to grease the cake form*

Glaze:
- *1 c. powdered sugar*
- *1 T. lemon juice*
- *1 T. boiling water*

Poppy seed roll

Rinse poppy seeds, scald with hot water and let sit overnight. The next day, prepare dough as for yeast-raised *babka* but a little more firm and let it rise.

Drain the poppy seeds in a sieve, grind at least three times.
Melt butter in a pot, add sugar, poppy seeds, honey, raisins, nuts and candied orange peel and fry a few minutes on a low flame, still mixing.
When slightly cooled, add egg whites whisked into a froth and mix.
Divide the dough and the poppy seed mixture into three parts.
Roll out each part of the dough, lightly sprinkled with flour.
Evenly spread poppy seed mixture on the dough, roll up the dough and place in long, approx. 18-inch loaf pans. The edges should be tucked under the dough roll.
Let the rolls rise in a warm place covered with a towel, then brush with an egg mixed with 1 t. milk.
Bake in a moderate oven (360°) for 35–40 minutes. Check if ready with a toothpick, which should remain dry. When slightly cooled, take out of the pans and glaze.

Ingredients:

Dough:
- 1 lb. flour
- 1 c. sugar
- $\frac{3}{4}$ c. margarine
- 3 egg yolks
- 1 c. milk
- 1 oz. yeast
- grated lemon peel (scalded with water)
- salt
- butter and bread crumbs to coat the forms

Filling:
- 1 lb. poppy seeds
- 1 c. sugar
- 2 T. honey
- 1 rounded T. butter
- 2 egg whites
- vanilla sugar
- $\frac{3}{4}$ c. raisins
- 1 c. chopped walnuts
- 1 T. finely chopped candied orange peel

Brushing:
- 1 egg

Glaze:
- 1 c. powdered sugar
- 1 T. lemon juice
- 1–2 T. boiling water

125

Honey-spice cake

*C*ream butter in a large bowl, add egg yolks,
sugar and spices and mix until smooth. Pour in liquid honey,
coffee and lemon juice and continue to mix for a while,
then mix soda with sifted flour. Add figs, orange peel, walnuts
and raisins to the egg-and-butter mixture and mix all together.
Beat egg whites into a froth and spoon alternately with spoonfuls
of flour into the mixture, still stirring.
Pour the dough into two loaf pans (10 inches x 5 inches)
greased with butter and sprinkled with bread crumbs, and place
them immediately in a pre-heated (300°) oven. When the dough
has risen, increase the temperature bake in a moderate oven (360°).
Do not disturb while baking for about 40 minutes.
Before taking out, check with a toothpic.
The toothpick should remain dry.
When slightly cooled, take out of the loaf pan.
Honey-spice cake will last as long as 2–3 weeks
tightly wrapped in aluminum foil.

Ingredients:

- 1 lb. flour
- 4 eggs
- 1 c. honey
- 1 c. sugar
- ½ c. butter or margarine
- 2 t. instant coffee
- juice of ½ lemon
- 1 t. baking soda
- 2 t. spices consisting of cloves, cinnamon, cardamom, pepper and nutmeg

- 2 T. chopped walnuts
- 2 T. finely chopped candied orange peel
- 2 T. figs cut into thin strips
- 2 T. raisins
- butter and bread crumbs to grease the loaf pan

Swets & Zeitlinger GmbH
Schaubstraße 16, Nähe Museumsufer
D-60596 Frankfurt/Main

Tel: +49 69 63 39 88/0
Fax: +49 69 63 14 216/7
Email: infoge@swets.nl
www.swets.nl

keks – Fruit Cake

30 dkg   mąki (flour)
15 dkg   masła (butter)
20 dkg   cukier puder ~~...~~ (vanilla cooking sugar)
5 jaj ~~(..)~~ (eggs)
2 łyżeczki proszku do pieczenia (baking powder)
20 dkg   bakali (walnut, rasin etc.)

ucierać   masło + cukier + jaja
dodawać   mąkę z proszkiem
Na koniec wsypać bakalie
Piec   ok. 1 godz   temp. 170°C
wstawiać   do   nagrzanego piekarnika

Smacznego!

a bowl.

...tter
.../baking
...a time,

... oven
...pick.
...ng and
...onds.

• *vanilla sugar*

129

Cheese cake

*Q*uickly knead dough from the listed ingredients,
roll in aluminum foil and leave in the fridge
for half an hour. Cream butter with sugar in a large bowl,
adding egg yolks, one at a time, still mixing. Grind the cheese,
add to butter-and-egg mixture, then add vanilla extract and mix until
smooth. Add candied orange peel and rinsed raisins.
Take out the dough from the fridge and halve it. Roll out one half
to fill the bottom of the cake pan, pierce with a fork here and there
and bake at 360° for about 25 minutes until light golden.
Form pencil-thin strips from the rest of the dough.
Whisk egg whites into a stiff froth and gently mix with the cheese
mixture, then place on the baked crust and arrange the dough strips
on top, forming a checkered pattern.
Brush with lightly beaten egg white.
Place in a pre-heated medium oven (about 360°) and bake
for 50 minutes. When ready, open the oven and leave it open
for a few minutes, then take out the cheese cake.
Remove from the pan when cooled.

Ingredients:

Dough:
- $\frac{1}{2}$ lb. flour
- $\frac{1}{2}$ c. margarine
- $\frac{1}{2}$ c. powdered sugar
- 2 egg yolks
- 1 grated lemon peel

Cheese mixture:
- $1\frac{3}{4}$ lb. farmer cheese
- $\frac{1}{2}$ c. butter
- 5 eggs

- $1\frac{1}{4}$ c. sugar
- vanilla extract
- $\frac{1}{2}$ c. raisins
- 2–3 T. finely chopped candied orange peel

Brushing:
- 1 egg white

Apple crumb cake

uickly knead dough from sifted flour and other ingredients, wrap in aluminum foil and leave in the fridge for half an hour. Peel and core the apples, chop and cook with 2–3 T. water. Add sugar, cinnamon, orange peel, cook a few minutes, still mixing, until it is a thick marmalade. Halve the dough. Roll out one part thin, place in the cake pan (10 x 10 in.), pierce with a fork here and there and bake at 360° for about 20 minutes until light golden. Take out of the oven, line the sides of the pan with some dough, sprinkle the baked crust with bread crumbs or crushed wafers and spread the marmalade on it. Make fingers from the rest of the dough and arrange them densely on the marmalade. Bake at 360° for 30–40 minutes. Glaze when cool. To make the glaze, mix powdered sugar with lemon juice and 1 T. hot water. If the glaze is too thick, you may add more water. When the cake cools completely, cut it into squares.

Ingredients:

Dough:
- 1 lb. flour
- 1 c. margarine
- 1 c. powdered sugar
- 2 egg yolks
- 3–4 T. sour cream
- vanilla sugar

Filling:
- 2 lb. apples (not sweet)
- ¹⁄₂ c. sugar

- 2–3 T. bread crumbs or crushed wafers
- 1 t. cinnamon
- 1–2 t. finely chopped candied orange peel

Glaze:
- 1 c. powdered sugar
- 1 t. lemon juice
- 1–2 T. boiling water

Walnut torte

Grease a round cake pan with butter and sprinkle with bread crumbs.
If your oven is large enough, best to bake two at a time.
Otherwise you can halve the ingredients and bake one after the other,
or else one high cake which will be sliced into two layers when cooled.
Cream egg yolks until foamy. Beat egg whites into a stiff froth and spoon alternately
with ground walnuts and wafer cookies to the cream, still gently mixing.
Pour immediately into the cake pan
and place into a medium oven (360°). Bake for about 20 minutes.
Do not disturb while baking. Check if ready with a toothpick.
If the toothopick is dry, the cake is baked and can be taken out.
Baked and cooled torte layers can wait overnight covered with aluminum foil,
but they can also be used just after cooling.

Filling: Cream butter with sugar. When the sugar is completely dissolved,
add a few drops of strong coffee, still mixing, and adding the egg yolks
one at a time. The filling is ready when $^1/_2$ of the coffee is added.
Mix the remaining coffee with the cherry liqueur and moisten the torte layers,
beginning from the bottom layer placed on a plate. Spread the filling evenly
over the bottom layer, then place the second layer on top of it and moisten it
with the remaining coffee and cherry liqueur mixture.

Glaze: Add 1 T. milk to the sugar, simmer on a very low flame, dissolve,
add cocoa powder mixed with the remaining milk and cook, still mixing.
When the glaze is completely smooth, take off the flame, add butter
and let it cool a little, still mixing. Cover the torte with the glaze, including
the sides, which may also be sprinkled with chopped walnuts.
Garnish the torte with halved walnuts and candied cherries.

Ingredients:

Dough:
- 1 lb. ground walnuts
- 4–5 ground wafer cookies
- 1 lb. sugar
- 10 eggs
- butter and bread crumbs

Filling and moistening:
- 1 c. butter
- 3 egg yolks
- 6 T. powdered sugar
- $^1/_2$ c. strong coffee
- 1 shot glass cherry liqueur

Glaze:
- 3 T. sugar
- 6 T. milk
- 2 rounded T. cocoa powder
- 1 t. butter

Garnish:
- a few halved walnuts
- crushed walnuts
- candied cherries

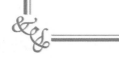

Filled doughnuts (pączki)

*M*ix the yeast with 1 T. sugar and a few T. lukewarm milk.
Cover with a towel and leave in a warm place. Sift the flour, add a pinch of salt.
Mix egg yolks with sugar until almost white, add to flour and yeast, pour in the rest
of the milk and the rum, and mix using a mixer until all ingredients are well
combined and the dough is smooth. When almost ready, slowly add melted butter
or cooking oil and candied orange peel. When the dough has absorbed all the butter
or margarine and comes off of the sides of the mixer, cover with a towel
and leave in a warm place to rise for about an hour.
When the dough has doubled in volume, roll it out into a $\frac{1}{2}$-inch sheet of
dough and cut out circles using a glass. Place a little jam on each circle, cover
with another circle, pinch the edges together well and arrange the doughnuts
evenly on a floured breadboard. When they rise a little they may be turned over.
Melt the lard in a low wide pot and check if ready, dropping in a piece of dough.
If it rises immediately to the surface and is nicely browned, you can drop in
the doughnuts, a few at a time so they do not stick together, bottom side up,
and slowly fry covered on a medium flame. Turn over browned doughnuts
and fry uncovered a little while. Take out ready doughnuts with a sharp stick
or a slotted spoon and place on a few paper towels to get rid of excess grease,
then cover with lemon glaze.

Glaze: Add $\frac{1}{2}$ c. water to sugar and simmer until threads can be drawn
from the spoon. Take off the flame, let cool and mix with a wooden spoon until
the mixture is white, then add lemon juice, and some warm water if needed,
to obtain the consistency of thick sour cream.
Doughnuts may be sprinkled with powdered sugar instead of glaze.

Ingredients:

Dough:
- 4 c. flour
- 2 oz. yeast
- 1 c. milk
- $\frac{3}{4}$ c. sugar
- $\frac{3}{4}$ c. butter
or margarine
- 6 egg yolks
- a pinch of salt
- 1 jar plum jam
(about 1 c.)
- 1 T. rum
- 2 T. finely chopped
candied orange peel

Glaze:
- 1 c. sugar
- juice of $\frac{1}{2}$ lemon

Frying:
- $1\frac{3}{4}$ lb. lard

Faworki or chrust

*A*dd egg yolks, 1 egg, baking soda, liquor, salt
and sour cream to the flour sifted on a breadboard. Knead the
dough smooth. Separate $\frac{1}{4}$ of the dough, cover the rest with a bowl.
Roll out the dough very thin, as this is essential for the quality of the
faworki. The dough should be as thin as parchment.
Cut the dough into 1-inch strips with a sharp knife, then cut the
strips at an angle into 4- or 5-inch pieces. Make an inch-long slot
in the middle of each piece and twist one end through the hole.
Proceed with the other quarters of the dough in the same way.
Arrange the ready *faworki* on a floured baking sheet
or breadboard and cover with a clean dishtowel.
Melt lard in a wide low pot. Begin to fry when the lard is well
heated, which can be checked by dropping a piece of rolled out
dough into it. It should expand rapidly and get light yellow.
Drop in the *faworki* a few at a time, turn with a wooden skewer
and take out when light golden. Place them on a layer of paper
towels to get rid of excess grease, then generously sprinkle
with powdered sugar and vanilla sugar.

Ingredients:

Dough:
- *2$\frac{1}{2}$ lb. flour*
- *3 egg yolks*
- *1 egg*
- *$\frac{1}{2}$ t. baking soda*
- *$\frac{1}{2}$ c. sour cream*
- *1 shot glass rum or vodka*
- *a pinch of salt*
- *1$\frac{3}{4}$ lb. lard for frying*
- *powdered sugar and vanilla sugar to sprinkle*

Wydawnictwo **Andrzej Frukacz**

Exlibris

Galeria Polskiej Książki

00-499 Warszawa
Plac Trzech Krzyży 16
tel. (22) 628-31-07, fax (22) 628-31-55

Recipes
ALINA FEDAK

Translation
MAŁGORZATA WALCZAK, MICHAEL JACOBS, *Letter*man

Photographs
G-M STUDIO
MAREK GERSTMANN, JERZY MALINOWSKI

The pictured courses were prepared by the Flik Restaurant.

Chef
MISROŁAW RESZCZYK

Food presentation by
ROMANA DANIEL

Editing
PaArt

Design
look STUDIO, ul. Wielopole 17, 31-072 Kraków, tel./fax 429-18-31

ISBN
83-87071-32-3

The photographers wish to thank
Rosenthal Wedgwood
Zepter Poland
Dom Handlowy „Banasik"
for graciously providing tableware.